The Girl Who Wrote Her Own Fairytale

by Lee DeNoya
with paintings by Angel Dominguez
forward by Morgan Llywelyn

The Girl Who Wrote Her Own Fairytale

by Lee DeNoya
with paintings by Angel Dominguez
forward by Morgan Llywelyn

Text and Concept © Lee DeNoya
Illustrations © Angel Dominguez
Design and Layout © Silas Toball

www.leedenoya.com

PALMETTO
PUBLISHING

Charleston, SC
www.PalmettoPublishing.com

The Girl Who Wrote Her Own Fairytale

First Edition

Hardcover ISBN: 978-1-64990-793-6
eBook ISBN: 978-1-64990-791-2

For Angel

And with gratitude
to the women who helped me
navigate my journey,
find my gifts,
and write my own fairytale.

The best writing has a quality of magic like that of the ancient alchemist; a whole cosmos is formed from a deceptively simple web of words. The Girl Who Wrote Her Own Fairytale shimmers with the wonder of a uniquely creative imagination. It's a novel… a fable, a dream, a prediction… to challenge the mind and excite the senses.

In a refreshingly new voice that defies categorization, Lee DeNoya welcomes you into a world that is both intimate and universal; a world unlike any other yet, hauntingly familiar. He invites you along on a voyage of exploration that ultimately leads to the discovery of Self.

Wait for a rainy day, seek a quiet corner, then settle down with The Girl Who Wrote Her Own Fairytale. This is a story to savor.

Morgan Llywelyn
Dublin, Ireland

StoryTime…

"Why do we read stories?" yawned the I-am-not-sleepy little girl.

Her grandmother asked back, "Why do you think? The characters? The worlds
they create? Maybe as a way to escape?"

"Yes," she replied through eyes full of sand. "Yes, all of that. And…"

"…we see our Self in the tale," her grandmother said like she knew it well.
"We seek ourselves in who we meet, and choose which bits to lose and keep."

"And why do they rhyme?" her granddaughter probed to stretch the time.

"Rhyming is song on a page," the girl half-heard her grandmother say.

"And why do the best stories have pictures?" the little girl whispered as
she drifted.

"Maybe to say what the words can't tell," her grandmother mused, more to
herself. "Together, they pave a yellow brick road that leads down your own
white rabbit hole to your own Neverland, where you clap fairies real at your
own Hogwarts, and cast your own spells to grant the best wish to ever
come true…

the hero in your tale is you."

ill you read it again?" yawned the little blonde girl.
"Just one more time? You read it so well."
I looked down at my darling Granddaughter that night,
    and as always, I felt my heart swell.
I can't help it you see. She reminds me of me–
    just as close as the Ring and the Bell.
So, a smile in my eyes, I reached out for my book
    and the story I most love to tell.

My hand went to the book, though I cast not a look,
    for it lay where I'd set it down last,
just the evening before, and the night before that,
    and each bedtime these several weeks past.
I turned each careworn page for my Granddaughter's sake,
    though my eyes were never downward cast,
but transfixed, by the light in my girl's bright green eyes,
    as I took us both back to the past.

er home stood where the trees meet the tireless sea
        and the wide-shouldered mountains stand tall,
in a village where people were born, lived and died
        never leaving their village at all.
A green, sentient place with such grandeur and grace,
        but to her everything was too small,
and the voice in her mind screamed the watchwords of youth–
        want it here, want it now, want it all!

An intelligent girl with a heart good as gold,
        she'd lived there since the day she was born.
She'd been nurtured by parents who loved her, and yet
        she'd recently been quite forlorn.
As a child she'd been happy, content just to "be"–
        not a single heartfiber yet torn.
But now, as she matured, a new voice in her mind
        left her angst-ridden, brim-full with scorn.

All the people around her seemed happy enough,
       as they had her whole lifetime, and yet,
to her eyes they looked passive, like sheep in the field.
       Every day she'd awaken and fret,
"Am I just going to lay here and settle for less,
       give up all that I've dreamt and forget
that the world's out there passing me by everyday!"
       Thus each day, she'd awaken upset.

"There's a big world out there with so much more than here,
       and I'm missing it!" they'd hear her say.
"I have all of this energy bound up inside
       but I'm rooted here day after day.
I will leave here tomorrow. To where I don't know,
       but I know that I'll wilt if I stay."
And with that, she decided she'd spend one more night,
       then be future-bound by break of day.

In the morning, the Young Woman shouldered her pack
and stepped into the freshening day.
She knew not where to go, but felt certain that
all of her answers lay somewhere away.
So she walked up the path that led out from her home,
to the road that would take her that day
on a journey, much different from what she had planned—
to a place not all go, but all may.

She strode straight up her path with eyes just for the end,
never looking at all to the side,
when a voice 'round the bend scratched, "What took you so long?"
She could not find the source, though she tried.
"I suppose you thought I would come looking for you?"
Then the Young Woman finally spied
an old woman who sat by the side of the lane,
looking sorely in need of a ride.

The old woman was clothed not in fin'ry, although
neither could one describe them as rags.
All around her, in front and behind and beside,
were all sizes and textures of bags.
This quite puzzled the girl, for the old woman looked
so unable to carry or drag
any fraction of what now surrounded her there.
So the Young Woman let her pace lag.

"Lovely morning, grandmother," the Young Woman called,
not yet halting, but shortening her stride.
"Can I help you somehow? I've a trip to complete
but perhaps I can find you a ride."
The old traveler looked the girl square in the eye.
Then she cracked a wry smile and replied,
"I do not need your help. 'Tis for you that I wait,
but I thought that you'd never come by!"

Just imagine the look on the Young Woman's face!
        She looked stunned and perplexed–yes, and more!
"You've been waiting for me? Well, I don't understand.
        See, I've only just walked out my door!
I have not told a soul in the world that today
        I'd be leaving. So please, I implore,
tell me how you can say you've been waiting for me
        when I've never seen you 'round before."

"I sit right here today as I have your whole life."
        "That's impossible!" cried the stunned girl.
"Many things seem impossible when one is young
        and one's life has not fully unfurled.
But one can learn the opposite," said the old dame,
        as she drew up her mouth in a curl.
"To the right combination of patience and drive,
        every oyster will yield up a pearl.

"You've just lived long enough now to notice me, dear.
        'Till today, right on past me you've flown.
Most will live their lives through and not hear my old voice,
        choose to listen, and make me their own.
Yet, although you're still young, you see me here today.
        'Tis in my view your chance to atone
for the hasty decision to walk out your door,
        toward a life you'll no longer postpone."

"There's no need to atone," the Young Woman replied,
        "I have great things to which I aspire.
There are talents inside me that yearn to be free,
        but they need to be sparked into fire.
Neither kindling nor flint can be found where I am.
        To be all I can be I require
a more challenging place to inspire my best,
        as the wind lifts an osprey up higher."

"If you would be the osprey, analogously,
　　　your perspective just needs to be shifted.
True, you have fine strong wings, searching eyes and quick wits.
　　　With an arsenal you have been gifted.
True, you could use your wings to soar high on the breeze,
　　　but rewards for the osprey are lifted
from beneath the sea surface, no matter the wind,
　　　no matter how high you have drifted.

"The Sea Eagles indeed have their traveling side–
　　　'cross a wide territory they roam.
To the north they will fly when they reach their first year,
　　　leaving wintertime's chill and seafoam.
But the osprey is like that great traveler of old,
　　　brave Odysseus, of the Greek poem.
His wide travels, of which my friend Homer has sung,
　　　were to bring brave Odysseus home.

"So it is with the osprey. Their lives are a blend
　　　of unequal parts work and romance.
Their great eyries necessitate steady repair
　　　due to their sea-exposed circumstance.
The male's work is near constant, the female's unceasing,
　　　with no time for extravagance.
Nearly blind to their work, we see only their flight.
　　　We'd trade places if given the chance.

"If you choose for your model the Sea Eagle's life,
　　　keep in mind that your work will not cease.
As you fly all directions for work or for play,
　　　your desire for home will increase.
Not a physical place. Not a house or a town,
　　　but a feeling of being at ease.
And the osprey has one other lesson to teach–
　　　let me tell you, then I've said my piece."

By this time, the Young Woman had heard 'bout her fill,
      and was eager to be on her way.
So, she shuffled her feet 'round the stones in the road,
      and tried hard to find something to say
that would help her to quickly take leave of this chat,
      while she still had the best of the day.
And she said, "Thanks, old mother, for your fine advice,
      but I really must be on my way."

The old traveler smiled as much inside as out
      when she saw the girl soon would depart.
She reached into a bag with a gnarled, sun-browned hand
      and she said, "Best have this 'fore you start.
If you're journeying far now in search of your life
      with no guidance save that in your heart,
this will help you to know the direction you go,
      though you'll not find your course on a chart.

"This old compass will show you your bearing worldwide.
      That should give you an adequate range
to go trooping around trying to find what you want.
      But I give naught. I only exchange.
What I have's come hard-earned. I give nothing for free.
      It's a practice that I'll never change.
May this help you maintain a true course while you seek,
      though from me, you'll at times be estranged."

The Young Woman thought, "That would be handy indeed,
      but I really have nothing to spare."
Then she thought of the pocketwatch back in her room—
      she could give that away without care.
That old watch always moved much too slowly for her,
      and she never made time to repair.
She ran back and retrieved it, completed the swap,
      then continued her trek to elsewhere.

he Young Woman went south, her new compass in hand,
    the old woman's words fresh in her mind.
She'd intended to get a quick start on the day,
    but the counsel had put her behind.
As she walked, she would catch herself shaking her head
    and she'd think, "I could not be that blind!"
How could that strange old woman have been there lifelong
    for the hurried Young Woman to find?

She crossed over the bridge on the south edge of town
    and walked on through the lowlands and fens.
Wetlands gave way in time to the wide rolling hills,
    separated by forested glens.
In expansive green meadows beneath azure skies,
    flowers waltzed with the elegant whins.
The road wandered the land at a leisurely pace,
    flowing riverlike, bend into bend.

Once well into this vista, the Young Woman felt
    hunger's tug for a late morning meal.
Her desire became irrepressible when,
    from a distance, the noontime bell pealed.
She moved off of the lane through a stand of fir trees,
    from the sun's heat her break to conceal,
and emerged from the trees at a wide meadow's edge.
    As a lunch spot, it held strong appeal.

She'd prepared several meals for her journey away
    and withdrew her provisions to start.
She then laid out the bread and the meat and the cheese,
    peeled her orange, divided the parts.
Just beginning to savor her favorite fruit,
    such a succulent taste, sweet and tart,
she glanced up, and discovered a person nearby.
    Quite a startle that gave to her heart!

At the edge of the meadow, not so far away,
        stood a woman with palette and brush.
She was dressed all in white from her cap to the ground,
        her face reddened by sun-fathered blush.
She was painting a scene of the meadow in Spring
        filled with sights, scents and sounds warm and lush.
Just behind her, a horse stood in front of a cart,
        half-concealed by the thick underbrush.

The Young Woman returned to her slices of orange
        and continued to lunch with some haste.
When she glanced up again, the Young Woman observed
        that toward her, the Artist now faced.
When her hunger was sated, she had some spare food,
        and since food is not something to waste,
she got up from her spot and progressed toward the cart,
        there, to offer the Artist a taste.

As she walked toward the Artist, her focus was drawn
        to the cart and the gray dappled mare.
She was slender and sleek for a cart-drawing horse.
        The Young Woman could not help but stare.
So as not to disturb the fine studio's peace,
        she approached the companions with care.
Then the Artist glanced up, gave a welcoming wave,
        and then ran her brush-hand through her hair.

"We were hoping that you would come over to chat
        and not think us standoffish or quaint.
If you offer that extra orange slice to my mare,
        I assure you, she'll give no complaint!"
"Does your mare have a name?" the Young Woman inquired,
        now relieved of the need for restraint.
"Since she's dappled with spots like the front of my smock,
        I thought nothing more fitting than Paint!"

Then the Artist guffawed and continued her effort
        to capture the charm of the day.
When the dialogue paused, the Young Woman glanced round,
        wishing now for no further delay.
In the cart there were canvases, every size,
        in a status of mild disarray.
The Young Woman perused them, and to her surprise,
        every one was done solely in gray.

Then she noticed the palette was gray edge to edge,
        and the canvas-in-process as well.
"How peculiar and wasteful," the Young Woman thought.
        "All that effort with nothing to sell."
Curiosity winning the battle with time,
        the Young Woman burst forth, "Please do tell,
why use only the gray and no color but that?
        Nothing bold? Neither prime nor pastel?"

"Oh, I used to use colors, the rainbow's full blend,
        to portray the world's beauty and grace.
But no matter my mast'ry of tinting and hue,
        my results were, to me, commonplace.
I could never quite capture what I had in mind,
        be it conflict or tender embrace.
Though my work was quite good, coming near to true life,
        the real thing, I could never replace.

"I would then show my work to the critics at large–
        the reputed experts of the day.
And I found myself reaping no joy from my craft,
        just frustration with what they would say.
Like so many before me immersed in their gift,
        like Fitzgerald, Mozart, and Manet,
critics dwelt on how they felt my work missed the mark,
        and I soon found my world wrapped in gray.

"Now I carry my true palette next to my heart.
        I'm immune to all those who'd embroil.
Color comes from inside, and the critics are moot,
        their obtuse negativity foiled.
As I journey, I paint and keep all in my cart.
        I feel only the joy, not the toil.
I use memory's palette to color the gray
        and give life to the monotone oil."

As the Young Woman followed the Artist's next stroke,
    she saw things as if seeing anew.
With the gray on the canvas, the Artist portrayed
    far beyond variation of hue.
She portrayed how all life forces interrelate,
    what the trees feel, and why the wind blew.
How the soil can breathe. That some birds fly for fun!
    Why young Dawn is so jealous of Dew.

At the top of the canvas, the Young Woman lunched
    as she had been scant minutes before.
"How'd you do that?" the Young Woman wondered aloud.
    "There was gray there before, nothing more!"
"It was there all along," said the Artist with pride.
    "Like a treasure behind a closed door.
Once you open the door, nothing happens by chance.
    It's amazing what life has in store.

"Like you choosing this meadow on this very day
    when I happen to be here as well.
Nothing random in that, yet what comes from our chat
    might take hours or years. Who can tell?
One can seldom know who one will impact the most
    in the time from hello to farewell.
But, you color your life from within all your days,
    it won't matter so much where you dwell.

"Let me give you a gift," the kind Artist proffered,
    turning briefly aside from her scene.
"My old oils and palette have violet and red
    and each shade you could want in between.
May they color your journey with primes and pastels,
    be your circumstance royal or mean.
May they help you draw subtlety from black and white—
    inspiration from grating routine.

Then the Artist's attention was back to her work
    as before the Young Woman appeared.
With the day mostly spent, the Young Woman walked home
    up the roadway from which she had veered.
The impression of her on the canvas behind,
    though still drying, would ne'er disappear.
For the Artist had captured her just as she was,
    whether traveling distant or near.

hen young Dawn next arose o'er the peaks to the east,
　　　bringing light to the Young Woman's view,
she looked out through her window to flowers in bloom,
　　　showing colors of every hue.
Her discourse with the Artist who paints all in gray,
　　　lay as fresh on her mind as the dew
t'would reveal every step she would take that bright morn,
　　　up the path she would choose to pursue.

Yesterday had not turned out the way she had planned,
　　　but today she would tarry no more.
She'd walk fast, far and strong 'till the sun went away–
　　　'till her journey-starved feet were both sore.
With her compass at ready, she set her course east,
　　　toward the mountains, away from the shore.
She strode confidently toward the pass through the peaks,
　　　knowing not what the day held in store.

She covered ground quickly from valley to foothill,
　　　from foothill to steep mountain pass.
All around her she noticed, as higher she climbed,
　　　a light sprinkling of snow on the grass.
The wildflowers and gorse were still shy with their blooms
　　　which down-valley had burst forth en masse.
Springtime's song grew much softer the higher she climbed.
　　　This was new to the untravelled lass.

She walked hard all that day, as the sun made its way
　　　from the Young Woman's face to her back.
Near the crest of the pass, the course widened a bit,
　　　and she sat down and opened her pack.
She enjoyed her late meal looking down at her town,
　　　feeling sure that she'd never go back.
O'er these mountains, she'd find the right place to provide
　　　all the chances her home village lacked.

As she sat there envisioning all that was good
        about every place other than home,
mixed with sounds of the wind blowing out toward the sea
        came a melody. No, just a tone.
It was so soft at first that she thought it imagined,
        or from far away had been blown.
But before long, she knew that it came from nearby.
        Like the volume, her interest had grown.

"Who is making that sound? No one lives way up here,"
        the Young Woman then heard herself say.
The words sounded quite loud to her sensitive ears,
        as she'd heard no one speak all that day.
As her ears sought the source of the sound, she could tell
        it was certainly not far away.
So the Young Woman packed up her gear and struck out
        toward the sound without further delay.

She had supped near the crest of the high mountain pass,
        so a few footsteps more brought her soon
to the path's highest point. Setting sun in the west,
        to the east was the rising full moon.
But her eyes lacked the interest to take in the view—
        such a visually breathtaking boon.
All her sensory energy went to her ears
        as they sought for the source of the tune.

Not a tune, she reflected. No tune—just a note.
        But a note like no other she'd heard.
The Great Poets would be at a loss to describe
        the emotional range this note stirred—
sheer delight at an infant's wide wonder-filled eyes,
        parents' mourning for illness uncured,
the discordant harsh jangle of coming of age,
        calm contentment from life's trials endured.

As the note sung out keenly between sun and moon,
        the Young Woman sought round in a rush
to find talent that with just one note, could convey
        soldiers' anguish and young maidens' blush.
As the Young Woman sought, the emotional score
        of the note grew increasingly lush.
Setting Sun touched his lips to the brow of the sea.
        The note stopped. Not a sound. All ahush.

No sound challenged the hush till the day-wearied disk
      settled into the sea for the night.
Then the note sang again, and she saw her at last,
      at the outermost edge of her sight.
The Musician stood tall at the brink of the void–
      at the cliff's edge, immune to the height.
So connected was she to the flow of the note,
      she had nothing left over for fright.

The Young Woman approached the Musician mid-note,
      then with trembling voice she did say,
"Would you tell me, Musician, with talent like yours,
      why a single note only you play?"
The Musician played on to the end of her bow.
      When the note was well-launched on its way,
she turned 'round and she gave the Young Woman a look
      with a poignancy hard to convey.

"Every day I play music for others who come
      to the concert hall, wanting to hear
the concertos and symphonies, operas and songs
      that for them lay a salve on their drear.
I'm the star of each solo–first chair violin.
      With my instrument, I'm without peer!
But the accolades brought by my work in the hall
      lack the power to comfort my tears.

"So each evening, I climb to the edge of this cliff
      and I play my note all the night through.
But for all of the energy spent at this ledge,
      none have seen me. Well, none except you.
For this note is mine only. I play it for me.
      I require no great maestro's cue.
I exhaust the anxieties, fears and distress
      that upon my soul, life has imbued.

"Like all others on Earth, I'm at war with my pain,
            and the most I can win is a truce.
So, I focus myself on my note every night
            in an effort to loosen the noose.
The events wrapped in joy often hold grief within.
            To imagine no pain is no use.
But while life without pain is beyond my control,
            my responses are all mine to choose."

The Musician's wise words touched the Young Woman's heart
            and she said, "Thanks for sharing with me.
I have not known your pain, but I do have my own–
            I know not where I'm destined to be!
So I'm leaving the village to find my true home.
            I don't know where it is, but I'll see.
I am confident that when I find the right place,
            ever after I'll live trouble free."

The Musician then smiled for the first time that night.
            Stepping forward, she tried to explain–
"If you open your heart to the love of this world,
            you'll be equally open to pain.
You're rewarded at times with immeasurable joy,
            while at others, you'll feel you've been drained.
Pain and Joy on this Earth are inseparable twins–
            Seek you Joy, you'll discover the twain.

"Please allow me to give you this flute as a gift.
            Keep it with you as you travel hence.
May it give you a note that you find is your own–
            one to lead you through fog, iron-dense.
You'll have times of great need, though you think not today–
            times when life seems to make little sense.
May this flute bring the peace that escapes me by day.
            All the pain from your soul may it rinse."

The Musician turned 'round, laid her bow to her strings,
            then proceeded to play to the night.
The full moon made her way 'cross the star-jeweled dome,
            casting all in a silvery light.
The Young Woman had hoped to continue her trek,
            but her weariness soon won the fight.
Village legend gave name to the heart-rending note–
            Mountain Keen, drifting down from the height.

The Young Woman awoke the next morning refreshed,
  gently brushed on the cheek by young Dawn.
She stood up in the light, wiped the dew from her face,
  stretched her body and savored a yawn.
On the damp turf beside her, she noticed her pack.
  Her new flute lay beside on the lawn.
All around her were remnants of last night's discourse,
  but the cliffside Musician was gone.

What the Young Woman heard on the mountain last night
  was still vivid in her memory.
That her progress had halted, she took as a sign,
  so she turned her path back toward the sea.
Making way toward the west, she would hire a ship
  that would take her where she could be free
to experience what had eluded her here,
  and discover her own destiny.

Time passed quickly that morning. She practiced her flute
  as she steadily worked her way down.
From the heights to the foothills, from foothills to valley,
  she finally reached level ground.
It took nearly all day to descend from the pass,
  and she said to herself with a frown,
"I've been seeking three days now and what have I gained?
  Here I stand, in the middle of town!

"If I'm ever to find the location I seek,
  my old ties with this place I must breach.
I will not spend the night here!" the Young Woman vowed.
  "I would sooner sleep out on the beach."
Though the sun would have kissed the cool sea on the brow
  'fore her night's resting place could be reached,
she set out toward the western extreme of her world,
  unaware of what that night would teach.

By the time she had made her way out to the sea,
    all was tinted with night's indigo.
As the temperature dropped and the moon crossed the sky,
    her anxiety started to grow.
She collapsed in despair in the lee of a dune,
    overwhelmed by disheartening woe.
Then, from out of the corner of tear-dampened eyes,
    she perceived an encouraging glow.

Down the beach she did hasten with quickening pulse,
    running hard, just as fast as she might,
toward a pale light behind a near-mountainous dune
    that obscured the glow's source from her sight.
When she rounded the dune, though she didn't yet know,
    she'd discovered an end to her plight.
Leaning casually back on a skiff turned keel up,
    sat a man in a circle of light.

The big man was a stranger with rough unkempt clothes,
    so her safety, as yet, was unclear.
Then, a gentle smile softened the lines 'round his eyes,
    and she felt she had nothing to fear.
"By my fire, come sit," the Explorer called out.
    "Warmth you need 'neath this sky cool and clear.
Then with Seasong and Starshine for fireside friends,
    not a reason you'll have for those tears."

"All my life I have lived here, just over those links,"
    sniffed the girl as she drew near the fire.
"I have never been so much as out of earshot
    of the bell in our village church spire.
So I'm leaving this valley and all I have known,
    but my prospects tonight appear dire.
For three days I've endeavored to strike my own path,
    but against me all seems to conspire."

"So 'tis off to the distance you're steering, you are,
    knowing not what you're going to find.
Seeking newness, you are, sailing close to the breeze.
    Charted waters you're leaving behind.
Such a thing as you do takes great courage, it does,
    for the winds can be harsh and unkind.
Wonderous places, there are, but to seek can become
    an obsession, consuming the mind.

"Much like you, once was I," the Explorer recalled,
    "looking ever for something without,
to come shake up my life and turn me to someone
    more heroic–not some nameless lout.
Seven seas I have sailed. The white whale did I seek.
    Gave blind eyes to all others t'would spout.
And when into my ears crewmen cried, 'Thar she blows!'
    'That's the wrong bloody one,' would I shout.

"Living hard though I was, gathering joy I was not.
    Not a soul wished to stand in my stead.
My own self did I ask, 'Why seek you what you seek?'
    and the answer rang out in my head!
'Seek I so I might find, it's the finding's the key!'
    And at that point, a different voice said,
'It's the steps on the journey, not reaching the end,
    that result in a life joyfully led.'

"From that day until this, traded vessels have I
    to a more satisfying design.
Not obsessed am I now with my destination,
    or with finding the treasure divine.
'Tis the journey I relish, so each dawning day
    is a treasure that I may make mine.
Well I rest then each night 'neath these flickering stars.
    In this way, I like they, burn and shine."

With that said, the intrepid Explorer laid back
        and gazed up at their personal sky.
"Lay we two here tonight 'neath this bowl full of stars,
        with those travelers from nights long gone by
who this way once have passed, on this spot settled down
        to take rest–down their burdens to lie.
Also with my true love, leagues away, who will see
        these same stars 'for tomorrow draws nigh.

"All the stars are eternal, they are, next to us–
        ever after and ever before.
Burned they have, and have shone, yet through all that occurs,
        true they are to themselves at their core.
Learn we can from the stars, if we keep them in sight
        as we travel through life seeking more.
They remind me, these stars, that the things we most need
        are not always the things we adore."

The Explorer then reached out and handed the girl
        a device that he'd had by his side.
"That's a sextant, that is," he explained to the girl.
        "Well it's served me for many a tide.
Give you bearings, it will, on your journey throughout
        this great world as you seek far and wide.
With that sextant in hand and the stars as your chart,
        from you no destination can hide."

The Young Woman was no longer crying. She knew
        that a power more certain than chance
had brought her to this beach, on this singular night,
        and presented this odd circumstance.
All the words she had heard these three frustrating days
        gave a lesson she'd missed at first glance.
Lifted now by the lightness she felt in her heart,
        'round the fire she started to dance!

The Explorer asked not why she danced as she did–
        only clapped out a rhythm in time
to the pace of the Young Woman's light dancing feet,
        wanting neither for reason nor rhyme.
They continued their fest all the way through the night
        until young Dawn had started her climb,
bringing end to the night that as long as she lived,
        the Young Woman thought her most sublime.

y the time that young Dawn had completed her climb,
　　　　the Young Woman felt lighter than air!
Though she'd danced the night through to the rhythm clapped out,
　　　　she felt fresh, energetic and fair.
She decided to promptly continue her trek.
　　　　To the village, she'd need not repair.
She said, "Thank you, kind sir, for refining my course."
　　　　Then they walked up the beach without care.

The Explorer soon wished her, "Brave journey!" and turned
　　　　toward the village for needed supplies.
Now enjoying the travel, she relished Seasong.
　　　　She no longer obsessed on the prize.
The Young Woman continued her walk up the strand,
　　　　bearing north, so the compass advised.
She would follow the beach to the forest's north edge,
　　　　there the rest of her course to devise.

She made steady headway, and soon came to the place
　　　　where the trees meet the tireless sea.
A sight brought her up short, and she said to herself,
　　　　"I can barely believe what I see!"
At the head of a path leading into the woods,
　　　　looking placid as someone could be,
sat the wizened old woman, complete with her bags,
　　　　nestled into the roots of a tree!

"'Tis the restless young osprey come down to the sea,"
　　　　quipped the woman from under the shade.
"Come, and sit down beside me and tell me, what's passed
　　　　since that day my acquaintance you made.
In exchange for recounting your travels thus far,
　　　　be they useful or sheer escapade,
I will share that last lesson the osprey can teach,
　　　　and we'll call it a fair and square trade."

"Well, I first met an Artist who paints all in gray
        but who colors her world from inside.
Then, a wondrous Musician who plays just one note
        as a comfort for pain she can't hide.
And last night, an Explorer with odd dialect
        gave me counsel by his fireside."
The old woman was pleased with the change she observed,
        but was not easily satisfied.

"He said bravery is needed by those who strike forth
        and set course for uncharted unknown,
and that spending one's life seeking only the prize
        can be wearying down to the bone.
All three gave me a gift that each hoped I could use,
        though their value has not yet been shown.
So, although I still journey away from this place,
        not so wistfully now have I flown."

The old woman said, "You are much better equipped
        than when I first appeared to your eyes.
And I'll venture to say there are lessons they taught
        that as yet you have not recognized.
Now, before you continue your journey away,
        one last lesson you'll hear, if you're wise.
It's a lesson best taught over seasons or years,
        but for progress' sake, I'll summarize.

"Each young osprey goes north, as I've told you before,
        at the end of their very first year–
just as you travel north on a trip of your own
        to see places you've never been near.
Then, upon their return to the place of their birth,
        they choose partners for life, to hold dear.
So their workload divides, and their joys multiply,
        and through vexation they persevere.

"But, paired off as they are for the rest of their lives,
        individuals they will remain.
While they work as a team on the duties at hand,
        their identities they will retain.
And with that, I've completed my part of our deal.
        Your advance I'll no longer detain."
With that said, the Young Woman took leave with the hope
        she would see the old woman again.

The Young Woman went north for the rest of the morn,
      reaching further and farther from home.
The great trees to her right sauntered down to the beach,
      so to soothe ancient roots in the foam.
As the sun reached its zenith, she stopped for a meal
      of dried mutton and sweet honeycomb.
Her night's sleeplessness caught her—adrenaline ebbed,
      and she laid her head down on the loam.

When she woke, she was facing the sea, and observed
      that the sun was now low in the sky.
She was rising to leave, but was taken aback
      by the sound of a movement near by.
"Who is there?" she called out, looking 'round ill at ease.
      And then promptly there came a reply—
"Only me," said a boy stepping into plain view,
      "just a traveler. A mere passerby.

"I was journeying west through the forest today,
      taking leave of my home 'cross the wood.
I had planned to progress to the edge of the sea,
      then turn one way or other for good.
When I came to this beach, I found you fast asleep
      and decided to help if I could.
So I paused on my way, to be sure you were safe.
      I hope I've not been misunderstood."

Not a boy, she now saw, having gathered herself—
      not a boy, but a handsome Young Man.
"Thank you for your concern, but I'm in no distress.
      Please come sit for a while if you can.
I'll be journeying north for the rest of the day.
      After that, I have no further plan."
And with that, she proceeded to clear off a space
      for the Young Man to sit on the sand.

The Young Man and Young Woman had similar goals,
       they discovered while chatting away.
Time slipped steadily by, (as it waits for no one),
       but the two noticed not the delay.
"It has gotten so late," the Young Woman observed.
        "Do you think we should go or should stay?"
The Young Man pulled a watch from his pocket to see
       how much longer they'd have light of day.

The Young Woman's green eyes grew as full as the moon
       that would soon be arising once more.
"That's my watch! Well it was. How'd it come to your hands?"
       the dumbfounded Young Woman implored.
"An old woman," he said, "by the side of the road,
       who I'd never laid eyes on before,
traded for my old compass that I never used,
       for I lack what it takes to explore."

The Young Woman reached into her pocket, and then
       it was his eyes that started to grow!
"She swapped me this old compass for that very watch
       which for me ran consistently slow!"
"Well it runs fine for me," the Young Man then explained.
       "It tells me what I most need to know–
every moment's a chance to be taken or lost,
       with a treasure I should not forgo.

"Since you're traveling north and, it seems, so am I,
       and we both can be nimble and swift,
why not travel together? At least for a while,
       so as not to feel quite so adrift."
The Young Woman agreed, and they strode up the strand
       as the tide was just starting to shift.
Every now and again, they would share the advice
       of their now complementary gifts.

THE END

ith the story completed, I closed the worn book
      and smiled down at my girl in her bed.
I expected the night would now come to a close
      since the favorite story'd been read.
But tonight, though she'd heard the tale dozens of times,
      questions whirled in my granddaughter's head.
Now she wanted to know more than words on the page,
      so she rolled over toward me and said–

"Then what happened, Grandmother? They walked up the beach,
      but that's really not much of an end!
Do you think that they traveled to far away places
      or went separate ways 'round the bend?
Did the Young Woman find a new place to call home?
      Did the Young Man and she become friends?
And the gifts she received from the people she met–
      what do you suppose happened to them?"

When the rapid inquiries came to a pause
      I said, "Well my inquisitive dear,
that day came to an end and turned into the next
      and turned weeks into months into years.
They took roads great and small on their travels abroad,
      and built courage to face down their fears.
Through excitement and boredom, adventure and chores,
      they shared smiles, and they cried a few tears.

"The two traveled through valleys and scaled many peaks
      while enjoying the path that they trod.
And ironically, they made a home for themselves
      back on very familiar sod.
They came back to the place where the trees meet the sea
      and the great-shouldered mountains stand broad."
Then I smiled to myself and distractedly mused,
      "Who'd of thought," and I started to nod.

"She went back to that village she hated so much?!
      I thought she really wanted to leave!
What about all those things that the Young Woman felt
      she was destined to have and achieve?"
To this question, I startled abruptly awake,
      and rocked out of my chair with a heave.
Then I dreamily said, "That's the part of this tale
      that I've always found hard to believe.

"We each weave our own fabric, unique in the world,
        as we work at life's loom every day.
We start simple, the color we are as our base.
        Some are blue, some magenta, some gray.
We spin thread from the teachings, the people, ideas
        that we choose as our guides on the way,
and develop a tartan that shows who we are,
        neverminding how widely we stray.

"Somewhere child, on her journey, she found there's no place
        that determines what comes of one's life.
One can conjure up joy from the meanest of states,
        or turn paradise quickly to strife.
She had taken for granted the liberty that
        in her village had always been rife.
So, her yearning to be somewhere else laid to rest,
        she'd found home, and became the Man's wife."

"If the Young Man and Woman got married and lived
        in the village where she'd always been,
what became of her great aspirations and dreams?"
        the girl asked with continued chagrin.
I just stood by her bedside, admiring my girl—
        so much drive and impatience within.
"It's at times such as these she reminds me of me,"
        was my thought as I widened my grin.

"We are all many people, just not all at once.
        Take a look at yourself and you'll see.
You're a girl and a daughter—a granddaughter too.
        You're a student, and yet you teach me!
As you grow, you'll become even more if you wish.
        You're in charge of your own destiny.
The Young Woman was wife and musician and mother
        and traveler and child of the sea."

"What'd she do with the gifts?" my girl pressed yet again,
      (for great patience was not one of hers).
The old clock said that I should stop talking, and yet,
      my girl's interest I would not deter.
For I knew that the day would arrive all too soon
      when my tales would no longer allure.
So, I answered the questions, assured that the child
      was myself in a young miniature.

"The Young Woman could find little use for the paints,
      but she keeps them for others who may.
The Musician's fine flute was a joy from the start
      and she plays it to this very day.
The old sextant, she passed to her second born son,
      for he sails the seas, turquoise and gray.
But each gift bore another she used her lifelong
      to stand up to life's trials and dismay.

"A gift's luster, when given, may be hard to see,
      yet it's value should not be dismissed.
Some appear to contain no real treasure at all,
      but they do, or they wouldn't exist.
Some seem more like a hindrance when first they arrive–
      you see no way that they could assist.
But all gifts have a value if used the right way.
      I guess that, my dear child, is the gist."

"Did the Young Woman see the old woman again?
      I was thinking for sure that she might.
And what ever became of the compass and watch?
      They were really important gifts, right?"
I leaned over the bed and I gave her a hug,
      sat back down, and then dimmed the girl's light.
"Those, my child, were the most precious gifts of all, but,
      that's a tale for a different night."